10 STEPS
to
Building Your First House

By: S.L. Blackwell

DISCLAIMER

S.L. Blackwell is in no way giving legal or business advice. These are the steps that were taken to start S.L. Blackwell's Builder business and are being shared to use as a guide while you do your own due diligence. Any company mentioned in this guide is used as an example and is not affiliated with S.L. Blackwell. Please do research for your state and only invest in your business what you can afford. This guide is no guarantee of your success.

ABOUT THE AUTHOR

Mr. Blackwell has been doing Real Estate since 2005. He started as a wholesaler, then started rehabbing, stepped up to doing new construction in 2015, and a few years later obtained his GC License. At the time of writing this book he has already completed over 40 construction projects. His mission is to help others and guide them on building homes themselves. He started a Builder Workshop in 2022 and also does 1 on 1 mentorship.

TABLE OF CONTENTS

INTRODUCTION

Welcome to "10 Steps to Building Your First House," a guide designed to lead you through the exciting and rewarding process of constructing your own home. Think of this book as your foundation, laying the groundwork for your journey into the world of building. Much like learning the basics in math, where you master addition before diving into more complex concepts, this guide will introduce you to the fundamental steps of building your home or investment home.

Just as 1 plus 1 equals 2, we'll start with the fundamental elements that constitute the construction process. As you progress through these steps, you'll gain the knowledge and confidence needed to take on more advanced aspects of home building. Consider this the initial stage of your education in the art and science of constructing a home.

I envision this book as the starting point in a series that will gradually delve deeper into the intricacies of building your house. Each volume will build upon the last, providing you with a comprehensive understanding of the entire process. The goal is to empower you to make informed decisions, turning your home into a tangible reality.

So, without further ado, let's embark on this journey together. Whether you're a novice eager to learn or someone with a bit of experience looking to refine your skills, this guide is crafted to meet you where you are in your home-building adventure. Let's dive into the first steps, and as we progress, you'll gain the tools and insights needed for the fulfilling endeavor of building your own home.

STEP 1: FINDING THE LAND

The initial stride in building your home is securing the right piece of land. Many enthusiasts embark on this quest without truly comprehending what to look for. Here's the cardinal rule: start by seeking flat land. Avoid the complexities of a decline, steer clear of the intricacies of a basement lot or the nuances of a crawlspace lot. Instead, aim for what we fondly call a "slab lot" – flat, straightforward, and the least headache-inducing option.

While it's true that you may occasionally need to bring in some dirt, we won't delve too deeply into that aspect for now. The key takeaway is to find land that is as level as possible, facilitating a smooth and efficient building process.

Where to Scout for Land:

Exploring potential plots can be an adventure in itself. Consider perusing realty websites like Zillow, Trulia, Redfin, Loopnet, and Crexi. Attend tax sales, seek recommendations from friends, or engage real estate agents who can provide tailored listings based on your specific criteria.

The 10% Rule:

Now, let's talk numbers. Adhere to what I like to call the 10% rule. If you estimate your future home's value at $300,000, limit your lot expenditure to 10% of that, which equates to $30,000. Of course, some factors may sway this figure, such as whether the land is already cleared and graded. A well-prepared lot might warrant a slightly higher investment, but let's keep it simple for now.

Eyes on the Prize:

Pictures and virtual tours can only reveal so much. Take my advice: physically go and inspect the land. Don't rely solely on online images or Google Street View when making such a significant decision. Walk the location, feel the ground beneath your feet, and envision your dream or investment home taking shape.

In essence, Step 1 is about laying the groundwork, both figuratively and literally. We're seeking simplicity in flatness, leveraging online resources, adhering to a budget, and, most importantly, trusting our instincts by physically surveying the land. So, put on your explorer's hat, and let's take the first step toward turning your home into a reality.

STEP 2: PRELIMINARY PAPERWORK

Now that you've secured your plot, it's time to dive into the essential groundwork preceding the permit phase. This involves a series of crucial steps, ensuring that you're well-prepared for the journey ahead.

1. Surveying Your Territory: The first task on your checklist is obtaining a thorough survey of your land. This step is the blueprint for what follows. A comprehensive survey not only outlines the boundaries of your property but also serves as the canvas upon which your investment or dream home will take shape.

2. Choosing the Right Floor Plan: Armed with your survey, the next step is selecting a floor plan that aligns seamlessly with the dimensions and features of your land. This crucial decision sets the stage for the entire construction process. The goal is to harmonize your vision with the practicalities of the chosen plot.

3. Crafting a Site Plan: Once you've chosen a floor plan, it's time to craft a site plan. This document details the placement of your future home on the land, considering factors such as access points, utilities, and landscaping. Think of it as the strategic guide for transforming your vision into reality.

4. Navigating the Permit Process: With your floor plan and site plan in hand, you're ready to tackle the permit application. Most locations don't require a land disturbance permit for plots under an acre, but it's crucial to check with your local planning and zoning department. Some areas may have specific requirements, even for smaller disturbances. Engage with the experts early on to avoid any surprises down the road.

Key Tip: Always consult with your planning and zoning department before proceeding. Their expertise will guide you through any specific requirements for your location, ensuring a smooth and compliant permit application process.

By completing these preliminary steps, you're not just checking boxes; you're building the foundation for a successful home construction project. The survey, floor plan, and site plan are the tools you need to navigate the permit process effectively. So, let's continue this journey, armed with knowledge and a well-thought-out plan, as we move closer to bringing your home to life.

STEP 3: CLEARING AND GRADING THE LAND

With your chosen plot in hand and the preliminary paperwork squared away, it's time to transform the raw potential of your land into the blank canvas for your home. This involves a crucial dance of clearing and grading, ensuring a smooth foundation for what's to come.

1. Clearing the Canvas: Start by surveying your land. If you've secured a flat lot, the grading process should be relatively straightforward. However, if nature has bestowed your plot with trees and shrubs, it's time to clear the canvas. Clearing involves removing obstacles, trimming back nature's excess, and creating a clean slate for your future home.

2. Grading for Perfection: Once the land is clear, it's time to grade. This step ensures that your plot is not just flat but precisely leveled according to the specifications laid out in your site plan. Your foundation contractors, armed with this plan, will work their magic, bringing the land to the desired level and preparing it for the next crucial steps.

3. Forming the Foundation: As part of the land-clearing and grading process, your foundation contractors will introduce form boards. These boards are the first tangible steps toward your home's foundation. They act as a guide, dictating the exact dimensions and layout outlined in your site plan. With precision and expertise, your foundation team will set the stage for the sturdy base upon which your dream or investment home will rest.

It's worth noting that this step is a collaborative effort between you, your contractors, and the site plan you meticulously prepared. As the form boards take shape, envision the blueprint of your home materializing before your eyes.

Key Tip: Trust your foundation contractors to interpret and implement the details of your site plan. Their expertise ensures that the groundwork aligns seamlessly with the vision you've set forth.

With the land cleared, graded, and the form boards in place, you're not just creating a foundation; you're shaping the very essence of your future home. Join me in the next step as we delve deeper into the intricate process of constructing the solid base upon which your dream residence will stand tall.

STEP 4: SLAB IN PLUMBING

Now that your canvas is set, it's time to infuse the groundwork with the vital infrastructure that will breathe life into your future home.

1. Identifying the Blueprint: As you drive through burgeoning neighborhoods, you might notice PVC pipes protruding from the ground and water lines standing tall. This visual symphony signifies the intricate dance of slab plumb roughing. Picture these elements as the silent architects, setting the stage for the seamless flow of water and utilities throughout your home.

2. Plumbing Precision: Your plumbing team takes the spotlight during this stage. With precision akin to a symphony conductor, they tap into the sewer and water lines, running a network of pipes that will soon weave through the heart of your home. This meticulous process ensures that, once the slab is poured, your plumbing infrastructure is ready and waiting, hidden beneath the surface yet poised to deliver essential services throughout your residence.

3. Future-Proofing the Infrastructure: Slab plumb roughing isn't just about the present; it's about future-proofing your home. Every tap, every pipe, strategically placed during this phase, anticipates the needs of your household, ensuring that the infrastructure is robust and ready for the demands of daily living.

Key Tip: Communication with your plumbing team is key. Make sure they have a clear understanding of your home's layout and your specific requirements. This ensures that the intricate network they weave beneath the surface aligns perfectly with your vision.

As the slab plumb roughing takes shape, your dream or investment home moves one step closer to reality. The unseen arteries of your residence are carefully laid, promising a seamless flow of utilities and a solid foundation for the steps that lie ahead.

Join me in the next step as we delve further into the intricate process of transforming the groundwork into the living, breathing space you've envisioned.

STEP 5: POURING THE FOUNDATION

With the groundwork meticulously set and the plumbing infrastructure silently weaving its way beneath the surface, it's time for the transformative act of pouring the foundation. Step 5 marks a pivotal moment, as your home begins to materialize in the form of a monolithic slab – a testament to both efficiency and durability.

1. Monolithic Magic: Picture this: the foundation and footing poured simultaneously, a process known as a monolithic slab. This streamlined approach not only enhances efficiency but also contributes to the structural integrity of your home. The foundation and footing become one, creating a robust base upon which the entirety of your home will rest.

2. Precision in Action: Before the pour commences, your foundation team engages in meticulous site work. Rebar is strategically placed, footings are carefully dug, wire fences are set, vapor barriers are installed, and gravel is laid – all essential components contributing to the stability and longevity of your foundation. This choreography, performed before your eyes, is a symphony of precision and expertise.

3. Foundation Unveiled: As the concrete flows, your home takes a tangible form. The foundation guys work their magic, ensuring that every inch is precisely executed according to the site plan and specifications. It's a moment where the vision you've nurtured and planned for starts to become a reality, solidifying the very essence of your future abode.

Key Tip: Stay engaged with your foundation team during this process. Communication is crucial to ensure that every detail aligns with your vision, from the depth of the footings to the placement of the rebar. This collaboration ensures that your foundation is not just functional but a work of art in its own right.

With the foundation poured, your home's footprint is etched into the ground, marking the beginning of a new chapter in your home-building journey. Join me in the next step as we explore the subsequent stages, bringing us closer to the realization of your home.

STEP 6: GETTING THE HOUSE DRIED IN

With the foundation solidified beneath your feet, it's time to usher in the next crucial phase: Step 6 - Getting the House Dried In. This step involves the meticulous assembly of the framework that will soon cradle the soul of your investment or dream home.

1. Framing the Vision: The first act in this symphony is framing. Like an artist sketching the outlines of a masterpiece, your construction team will frame the skeleton of your home. Walls rise, spaces take shape, and the essence of your vision becomes tangible.

2. Roofing and Sheathing: Once the framing is complete, it's time to crown your creation. Roofing materials will shield your home from the elements, while sheathing – the sturdy plywood wrapping around your house – provides both support and insulation.

3. Wrapping It Up: Before the final touches, a vital step comes into play: the vapor barrier. House wrap, as it's commonly known, acts as a protective shield, ensuring that moisture stays out. This essential layer guards against the elements, preserving the integrity of your home.

4. Windows and Doors: As the walls rise and the sheathing embraces your home, it's time to invite the outside in. Windows and doors take their place, transforming mere openings into portals that connect your living space with the world beyond.

5. Dry It In: Once the windows are in, the doors are secured, the roof stands tall, and the sheathing envelops your home, you've achieved the milestone of "drying in" your house. Rain may dance on the roof, but it won't breach the fortress you've built. Your home is protected, and the interior is shielded from the elements.

Key Tip: Stay involved during this phase, ensuring that the framing aligns with your vision, the roof complements your aesthetic preferences, and the windows and doors enhance the overall design. This is your chance to see your dream taking shape, both inside and out.

As we conclude Step 6, your home is now sheltered and protected. Join me in the next step as we explore the intricate stages that follow, bringing us one step closer to the complete realization of your vision.

STEP 7: ROUGH MECHANICALS

With the framework in place and your home safely sheltered, it's time to breathe life into your dream space. Step 7 marks the initiation of the rough mechanicals – a crucial phase encompassing HVAC, plumbing, and electrical work.

1. HVAC Takes the Stage: The show begins with HVAC, the heavyweight of the rough mechanicals. Ductwork snakes its way through the skeletal structure of your home, and the furnace takes its place, laying the groundwork for optimal climate control. Tackling HVAC first is a strategic move; it's easier for plumbers and electricians to navigate around HVAC material than the reverse.

2. Plumbing Precision: Following HVAC, plumbing steps into the spotlight. Pipes wind their way through the structure, ensuring that water flows seamlessly to every corner of your home. This phase involves connecting the vital lifelines that will sustain your household – a choreography of pipes and fixtures taking shape within the walls.

3. Electrical Illumination: As the plumbing finds its path, it's time to illuminate your dream space. Electrical work commences, with wires weaving through the framework like a nervous system connecting every part of your home. Outlets, switches, and fixtures take their places, casting a glow that will soon bring your living spaces to life.

4. Rough Mechanical Harmony: Together, these three elements

– HVAC, plumbing, and electrical – create the symphony of rough mechanicals. Each system intertwines with the others, harmonizing to ensure the seamless functionality of your home. It's a dance of precision, with every element strategically placed to support and complement the others.

Key Tip: Coordination is key during the rough mechanicals phase. Communication between HVAC, plumbing, and electrical teams ensures that each system integrates seamlessly, preventing conflicts and ensuring the efficient operation of your home.

As we wrap up Step 7, your home is now infused with the essential systems that will make it a haven. Join me in the next step as we delve into the finishing touches that will bring your home to its complete and magnificent realization.

STEP 8: INSULATING YOUR HAVEN

With the foundational systems in place, it's time to cocoon your investment or dream home in a layer of comfort. Step 8 unfolds the insulation phase – a meticulous process of enveloping your living spaces in a shield against the elements.

1. Wall Insulation: The first act in this phase is wall insulation. Every exterior wall, every surface touching the outside realm, becomes a canvas for this essential layer. As the insulation takes its place, it forms a barrier, keeping your home warm in winter, cool in summer, and shielding it from the unpredictable forces of nature.

2. Attic and Knee Walls: Attention extends beyond just the walls. Any space touching the outside – including attic spaces and knee walls – demands its own coat of insulation. This ensures that every nook and cranny of your home maintains a consistent and comfortable temperature.

3. Patience for Ceilings: While the walls and designated spaces receive their insulation, the ceiling remains untouched for now. The reason lies in the delicate dance with drywall. Ceiling insulation, often blow-in, awaits its turn until after the drywall installation, ensuring a seamless and efficient process.

Key Tip: Precision is crucial during insulation. Ensure that every inch of the exterior walls and designated spaces is covered, providing a uniform layer that contributes to both comfort and energy efficiency.

As the insulation wraps your home in a cozy embrace, join me in the next step as we explore the transformative act of installing the finishing touches – bringing us one step closer to the complete realization of your home.

STEP 9: DRYWALL INSTALLATION

With the insulation cocooning your home, it's time for Step 9: Drywall Installation – the transformative act of crafting the interior canvas of your dream space.

1. Interior Transformation: As the insulation settles into its role as a guardian of comfort, the interior takes center stage. Drywall becomes the artist's brush, sweeping across the framework, shaping the contours of your living spaces. Every room, every corner, begins to define itself within the walls.

2. Precision in Placement: Drywall installation is an art of precision. Each panel is meticulously placed, creating a seamless surface that sets the stage for the texture and color that will soon breathe life into your home. This phase requires the skillful hands of craftsmen who understand the importance of a smooth and flawless finish.

3. The Unveiling of Rooms: As the drywall takes shape, rooms begin to unveil themselves. Spaces that were once defined by bare framework now assume the form of bedrooms, living areas, and the heart of your home – the kitchen. It's a moment where the potential you envisioned begins to manifest in tangible, touchable reality.

Key Tip: Stay involved during the drywall installation, ensuring that every seam is expertly sealed and every surface is primed for the next step. This phase is pivotal in laying the foundation for the aesthetic appeal of your interior spaces.

As the drywall wraps your home in a clean and crisp finish, join me in the next step as we explore the transformative act of adding color, texture, and personality to your dream home.

STEP 10: INTERIOR FINISH

With the drywall creating a blank canvas, it's time for the grand finale – Step 10: Interior Finish. This is the transformative act that turns your structure into a home, infusing it with color, texture, and the unique essence that makes it uniquely yours.

1. **Trim as the Finishing Touch:** The finishing touch comes in the form of trim. Doors, baseboards, crown molding, and other architectural details add a layer of sophistication, framing each room and completing the visual harmony of your interior spaces.

2. **Painting the Canvas:** The first stroke of the interior finish is the paintbrush. Colors you've carefully chosen dance across the walls, setting the tone for each room. This act of personalization turns your living spaces into a reflection of your taste, style, and the ambiance you desire.

3. **Cabinets and Countertops:** Next, your dream kitchen takes shape. Cabinets find their place, and countertops become the workspaces where culinary creations will unfold. This phase blends functionality with aesthetics, creating a heart for your home.

4. **Flooring Underfoot:** The soul of each room is encapsulated in the flooring. Whether it's the warmth of hardwood, the plushness of carpet, or the sleekness of tile, your choice of flooring completes the visual and tactile experience of your living spaces.

5. **Mirrors, Vanities, and Fans:** As the interior finish

progresses, mirrors reflect the personality of each room, vanities offer a touch of luxury to your bathrooms, and fans provide both comfort and a gentle breeze. Every detail, meticulously chosen, contributes to the holistic design of your home.

6. **The Culmination:** With the installation of the last detail, the culmination of your home-building journey is at hand. The dream you envisioned, planned, and built is now a reality. Your home is not just a structure; it's a testament to your vision, a haven crafted for comfort and joy.

Key Tip: During the interior finish, attention to detail is paramount. Take the time to ensure that every element, from the smallest knob to the grandest countertop, aligns with your vision and enhances the overall aesthetic of your home.

As you stand back and admire the completed masterpiece, revel in the realization that your home is now a tangible, lived-in reality. Congratulations, you've reached the end of your home-building journey.

CONCLUSION

In just 10 straightforward steps, you've embarked on a journey to build your own house. Let's quickly recap:

1. **Find the land.**

2. **Navigate preliminary work until securing the permit.**

3. **Clear, grade, and set the form boards for your land.**

4. **Implement slab plumbing.**

5. **Execute foundation work and pour the slab.**

6. **Achieve a dried-in house.**

7. **Tackle rough mechanicals.**

8. **Insulate your home.**

9. **Install drywall.**

10. **Complete the finishing touches with the interior finish.**

This beginner's guide has provided you with the fundamental steps to construct a home from scratch. As you've journeyed through these stages, you've gained insights into the artistry and precision required in each step of the process.

But the learning doesn't stop here. Anticipate a more in-depth exploration in the upcoming second edition, where we'll delve into each step, offering a richer understanding of how to master the art of building your own home from the ground up.

Thank you for joining us on this initial adventure. Stay tuned for the next edition, where we'll continue teaching you the intricacies of creating not just a house, but a masterpiece – your very own liveable art.